HOW DO YOU SPELL
UNFAIR?

MacNolia Cox and the National Spelling Bee

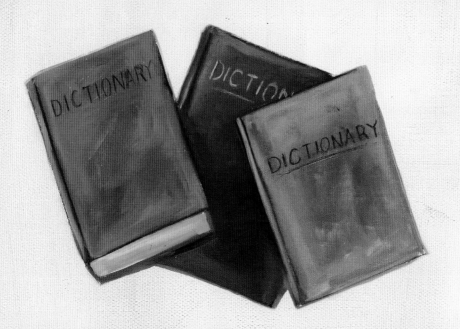

CAROLE BOSTON WEATHERFORD

illustrated by FRANK MORRISON

CANDLEWICK PRESS

*For every kid who's ever broken a spelling rule or had
their name misspelled or mispronounced.
And in honor of my mother, who drilled me for spelling tests,
and my dad, whose spelling dictionary is my well of words.*
CBW

To my bottle-of-energy grandson Miro—my man
FM

Text copyright © 2023 by Carole Boston Weatherford
Illustrations copyright © 2023 by Frank Morrison

First edition 2023

Library of Congress Catalog Card Number 2022908641
ISBN 978-1-5362-1554-0

23 24 25 26 27 28 CCP 10 9 8 7 6 5 4 3 2 1

Printed in Shenzhen, Guangdong, China

This book was typeset in Avenir.
The illustrations were done in oil and spray paint.

Candlewick Press
99 Dover Street
Somerville, Massachusetts 02144

www.candlewick.com

FOREWORD

♦♦♦

THE SCRIPPS NATIONAL SPELLING BEE is a big event. Contestants representing diverse cultures and nationalities look like a little United Nations. But spelling bees were not always open to anyone who could rise through the ranks. In areas where segregation was the law, citywide spelling bees were whites-only.

The first time that Black and white spellers competed nationally, the white grown-ups were sore losers. In 1908's National Education Association Spelling Bee, fourteen-year-old Marie Bolden, a Black girl from Ohio, led her team to defeat competitors from other cities around the country, including the all-white team from New Orleans.

A writer for the New Orleans *Picayune* newspaper claimed that Marie—who correctly spelled four hundred words in writing and another one hundred words orally—had bested white spellers because they were distracted by her presence. Angry white readers wrote to the *Picayune* calling for the school superintendent to be fired for putting white students in such an embarrassing situation.

But for Booker T. Washington, the famous African American educator, Marie's achievement was a sign of progress. "You will admit that we spell out of the same spelling book that you do," he said. "And I think you will admit that we spell a little better."

If Black children out-spelled whites in competition, it would prove that Blacks were just as smart as whites and were not inferior, as racists contended. And that's exactly why Blacks were barred from many local spelling bees. There would not be another Black finalist at a national spelling bee until 1936. This is her story.

MACNOLIA COX was no ordinary kid.
Her idea of fun was reading the dictionary.
From *A* to *Z*, she learned words' meanings and spellings.
She loved to read, study, and spell.

In 1936, the eighth grader won her school spelling bee.
After MacNolia passed a fifty-word written test
and an oral competition, she advanced
to the *Beacon Journal* newspaper's citywide bee.

That April evening, MacNolia faced fifty of the city's best spellers.
Three thousand people jammed the armory in Akron, Ohio.

Can you spell *nervous*?

N-E-R-V-O-U-S

With butterflies in her stomach and a lump in her throat,
MacNolia listened to pronunciations and definitions
before spelling each word. MacNolia got ruled out.
Teary-eyed, she got her coat and hat
and prepared to go home.
But someone urged her to stay.
Due to an error, the judges brought her back.
MacNolia correctly spelled *daft, writ, pretentious, brusque,
abstemious, gradate, felicitate,* and *apoplexy.*

Can you even pronounce those words?

In the final rounds of the bee, MacNolia battled
back and forth with John Huddleston
until he tripped up on the word *sciatic*.
After spelling the word that John had missed,
MacNolia had just one more word to the title—
voluble:
V-O-L-U-B-L-E.

With those seven letters, MacNolia became
the first African American to win the Akron spelling bee.
Her prize was twenty-five dollars and a trip
to the National Spelling Bee in Washington, DC.

Can you spell *surprised*?
S-U-R-P-R-I-S-E-D

At events all over Akron, MacNolia was the guest of honor.
Backstage at the Palace Theatre, the spelling dynamo
met dancer and actor Bill "Bojangles" Robinson
and jazz musician and composer Fats Waller.

At the Akron City Club, she dined with local bigwigs.
African American clubs held fundraisers,
and Black churches took up offerings to help
with her travel costs. People also prayed for her.

Akronites now mentioned MacNolia Cox
in the same breath as the boxing champion Joe Louis
and the track star Jesse Owens.

Letters and telegrams poured in from far and wide.
MacNolia's school community was rooting for her, too.
Her teacher, Miss Greve, bought her a new dress,
and a man gave her a beautiful necklace.

MacNolia also received two dictionaries to study.
She spent three periods a day prepping for the national bee.
She memorized one hundred thousand words!

Can you spell *dedication*?
D-E-D-I-C-A-T-I-O-N

At Akron's Union Station,
a military band and a crowd of thousands
saw the spelling champ off to Washington.
For her first train ride, MacNolia got on board
with her mother, Miss Greve, and Mabel Norris,
a reporter from the *Beacon Journal*,
the newspaper that sponsored the Akron bee.
"This is the most fun I've ever had," said MacNolia.

Can you spell *excited*?
E-X-C-I-T-E-D

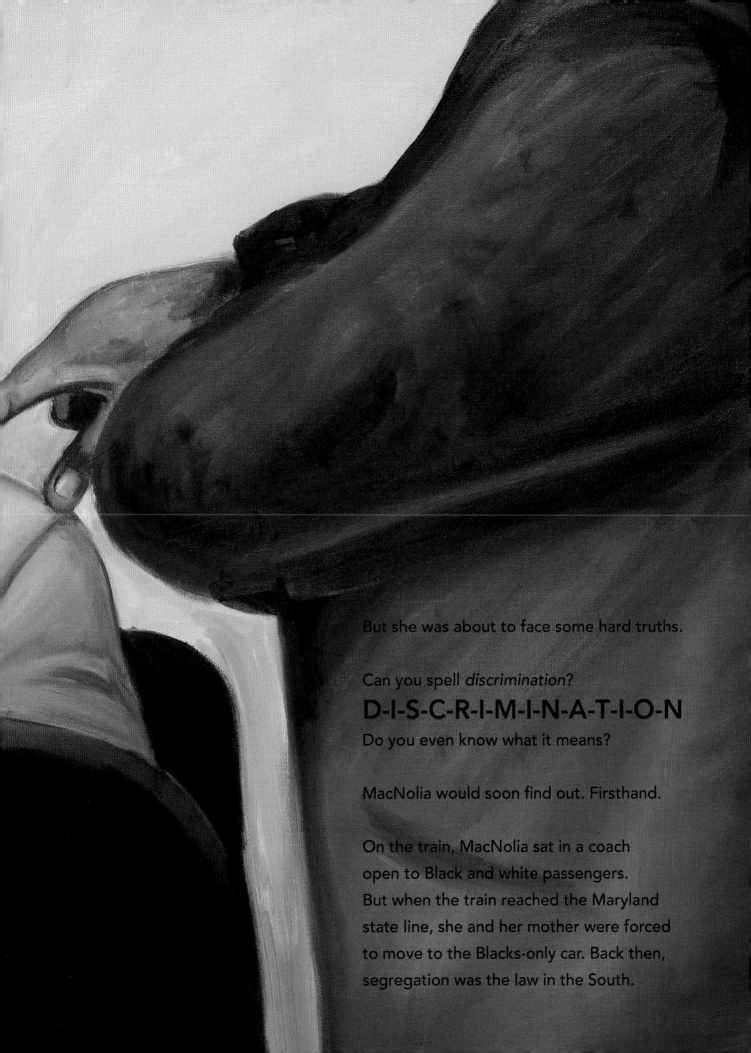

But she was about to face some hard truths.

Can you spell *discrimination*?
D-I-S-C-R-I-M-I-N-A-T-I-O-N
Do you even know what it means?

MacNolia would soon find out. Firsthand.

On the train, MacNolia sat in a coach
open to Black and white passengers.
But when the train reached the Maryland
state line, she and her mother were forced
to move to the Blacks-only car. Back then,
segregation was the law in the South.

When MacNolia arrived in Washington, she and her mother had to stay with a Black doctor because the hotel where the other spellers stayed was for white customers only.

MacNolia and her mother couldn't even ride the main elevator at the spelling bee banquet. They had to climb the stairs. Inside the banquet hall, they were seated away from the other spellers and their families.

She and Elizabeth Kenney, from Plainfield, New Jersey, were the first African American students to compete at the National Spelling Bee since nine newspapers founded the competition in 1925.

The two Black girls had to enter the ballroom through a back door and were seated at a card table apart from the other spellers.

Can you spell *racism*?
R-A-C-I-S-M

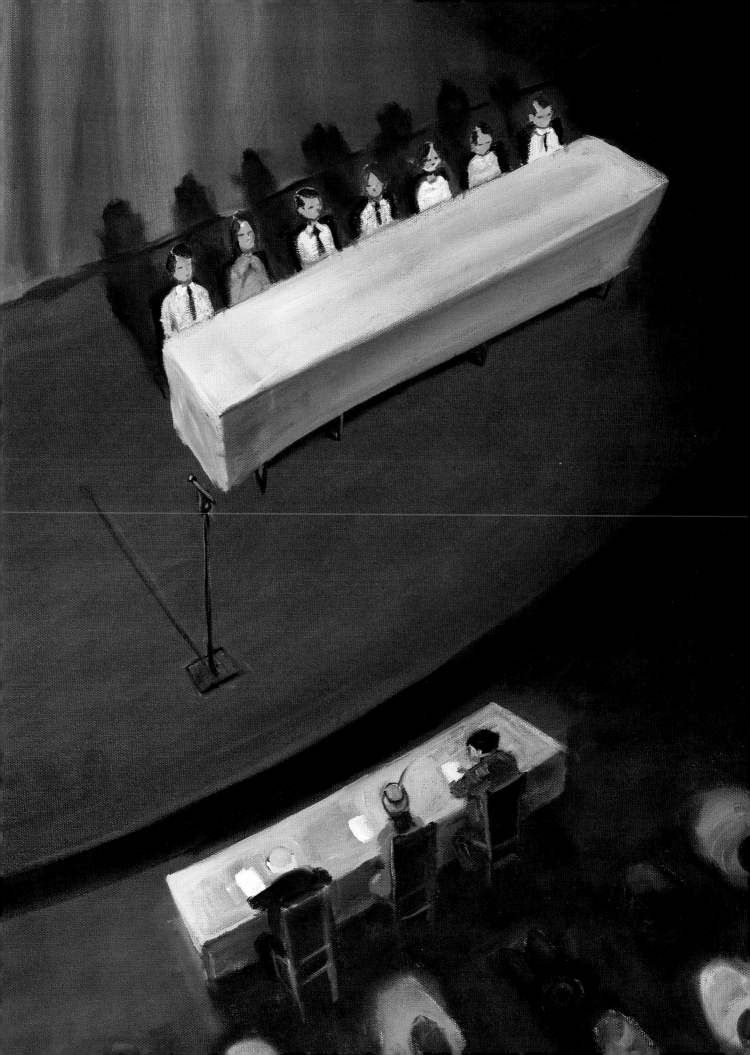

Though second-class treatment met her at every turn,
MacNolia couldn't afford to get rattled.
She had to concentrate and to believe in herself.
She remained calm and nailed word after word.

Can you spell *focus*?
F-O-C-U-S

The judges threw harder and harder words at the spellers.
In the audience, Miss Greve, MacNolia's teacher, bit her lip.
One by one, the competition fell.
Elizabeth Kenney misspelled *appellation* and placed tenth.
When Doris Rubin misspelled *acceptability*,
MacNolia advanced to the final five.

The judges, mostly from the segregated South,
couldn't seem to stump her.
Then they threw a curveball,
a word that MacNolia hadn't studied—
nemesis.

N-E-M-A-S-I-S, she answered.

MacNolia's teacher and the newspaper reporter protested. They argued that the word *nemesis* was not on the official list. Furthermore, in MacNolia's dictionary, the word was a proper noun— referring to a Greek goddess—and thus not acceptable. The judges stood by their decision.

Can you spell *unfair*?
U-N-F-A-I-R

MacNolia. Was. Out.
But what an achievement!
She had made history by becoming
a finalist in the National Spelling Bee.

The spellers spent the rest of
the week sightseeing.
They visited the White House
and the Washington Monument.
MacNolia saw stamps being printed
at the Bureau of Engraving.

Can you spell *amazed*?
A-M-A-Z-E-D

At the end of the whirlwind trip,
MacNolia took home a seventy-five-dollar prize
and was honored with a big homecoming parade.

Can you spell *proud*?
P-R-O-U-D

Even though she didn't win the championship,
MacNolia had proven that African American
students are as smart as anyone and can compete
and excel when given a level playing field.

That was MacNolia's triumph.

EPILOGUE

♦♦♦

MacNolia Cox was smart enough to excel at any career. However, she could not afford to attend college and wound up working as a maid for a doctor. She died in 1976 at age fifty-three.

The fight to integrate spelling bees did not start with Cox. Nor did it end with her. Since the early twentieth century, Black students competed in separate spelling bees. In Alabama, there was even a statewide Black spelling bee funded by African American businessman A. G. Gaston.

But the winners of those all-Black contests were not allowed to compete in the regional bees, a required step to qualify for the national championship. Nevertheless, African American students shone in the all-Black bees.

In December 1961, a notice about the upcoming bee sponsored by Virginia's *Lynchburg News* went out to local schools, including, mistakenly, the all-Black ones. A later letter corrected the error and withdrew the invitation, stating that Black schools were not expected to participate.

The Lynchburg branch of the National Association for the Advancement of Colored People (NAACP) got involved in the matter. The civil rights organization had waged the legal battle against school segregation that led to the landmark *Brown v. Board of Education* case. In 1954, the US Supreme Court had ruled that "separate but equal" schools were unconstitutional—against the law. The Lynchburg NAACP contacted the Scripps-Howard newspaper publishing group, the sponsor of the national spelling bee. The NAACP's letter pushed the newspaper publisher to open local spelling bees to all students, regardless of skin color. The NAACP also threatened the publisher with bad press and legal action for letting spellers from segregated bees rise to the finals. Scripps-Howard replied that local newspapers and schools set their own rules.

In 1962, George F. Jackson, a student from Lynchburg, wrote to President John F. Kennedy: "I am a thirteen-year-old colored boy and I like to spell. Do you think you can help me and get the Lynchburg bee open to all children?" The letter ran in newspapers across the country.

Like segregated schools, local spelling bees were slow to integrate. But as other racial barriers fell, local spelling bees opened to African Americans. In 1962, twelve-year-old Jocelyn Lee became the first Black winner of the Oklahoma City bee. And in 1965, fifteen-year-old Clorrine Jones won the first integrated bee to be held in Memphis, Tennessee.

In 1998, Jody-Anne Maxwell, from Jamaica, became the first person of African descent to win the Scripps National Spelling Bee.

In 2021, fourteen-year-old Zaila Avant-garde became the first African American to win the Scripps National Spelling Bee. The winning word was *Murraya*, the name for a genus of tropical trees. That same year, the US Senate passed a resolution honoring MacNolia Cox's life, legacy, and achievements.

SELECT BIBLIOGRAPHY

◆◆◆

Akron Beacon Journal, February 15, 1936–June 1, 1936. Accessed via Newspapers.com.

"A Brief History of Spelling Bees in America." Ford's Theatre. https://www.fords.org/blog/post/a-brief-history-of-spelling-bees-in-america/.

Cramer, Maria, and Alan Yuhas. "Zaila Avant-garde Makes Spelling History, and Other Moments from the Bee." *New York Times*, July 9, 2021. https://www.nytimes.com/2021/07/09/us/zaila-avant-garde-spelling-bee-winner.html.

"Elizabeth Kenney Survives 20 Rounds before Elimination in Spelling Bee." *Courier-News* (Plainfield, NJ), May 27, 1936, 10. Accessed via Newspapers.com.

Price, Mark J. "1936 Akron Spelling Champ Blazed Trail for 2021 Winner." *Akron Beacon Journal*, July 11, 2021. https://www.beaconjournal.com/story/news/2021/07/11/1936-akron-spelling-champ-blazed-trail-2021-national-winner/7932212002/.

"Senate Passes Portman, Brown Bipartisan Resolution Honoring North east Ohio Native, MacNolia Cox." Rob Portman, US Senate, press release, September 16, 2021. https://www.portman.senate.gov/index.php/newsroom/press-releases/senate-passes-portman-brown-bipartisan-resolution-honoring-northeast-ohio.

"Survey of the Month: Spelling Bee." *Opportunity* 14, no. 6 (June 1936), 185–186. https://archive.org/details/sim_opportunity-a-journal-of-negro-life_1936-06_14_6/page/184/mode/2up?q=macnolia/.

"Thirteen-Year-Old Akron Girl Wins Spelling Bee over 100,000 Pupils." *Pittsburgh Courier*, May 2, 1936, 1. Accessed via Newspapers.com.

"2015 MacNolia Cox Spelling Bee." *Urban News*, June 11, 2015. https://theurbannews.com/lifestyles/2015/2015-macnolia-cox-spelling-bee/.